Cleaning

2 towels
soap (in container)
and face cloth
⎫
paste and
⎪ Keep in a
⎬ strong plastic
rush, comb
metal mirror or polythene
⎪ bag
rush
shoe cleaning kit ⎭

Wearing (in addition to those being worn)

raincoat, anorak or cycle cape
spare shirt, shorts or dress
or jeans (2 of each)
spare underclothes (2 sets)
2 or 3 pairs socks or tights
gum boots and canvas shoes
strong shoes
warm jerseys or pullovers
coat hangers are very useful, and
also polythene bags for dirty clothes

Miscellaneous

box of tissues
notebook and pencil, crayons, etc.
camera and films
penknife
swimsuit
small plastic bags (are useful for
collecting things)
maps
books to read

Contents

Camping

by DAVID HARWOOD BA
illustrations by ERIC WINTER
cartoons by MARTIN AITCHISON

Ladybird Books Ltd Loughborough 1977

Camping

Before man learnt how to build houses, he lived in shelters which he made from whatever materials he could find, or he made a home in a cave. He was a natural

The Caveman was a natural camper . . .

camper. There are still millions of people in the world who spend all their lives outdoors.

As time went on, villages grew up, then towns and cities. People became used to living in properly-built houses, and only soldiers camped. It was not until this century that people began to camp because they wanted to. In the last twenty to thirty years camping has become more and more popular.

Modern camping can be great fun—or it can be a miserable experience. Some people do not like living outdoors and others are naturally attracted to the outdoor life. There are also people who have never been camping, or who have camped once and were disappointed because they did not know how to camp in comfort. In this book there are many hints and ideas on how to camp, and how to make the most of the opportunities which camping offers.

Tents

There is a wide choice of tents available, ranging from small two-man hike tents to large luxury frame tents which are almost miniature houses. What tent or tents you buy will depend on where you are going, how you are going to get there, and how much you can afford.

The tent is your most important item because it will be your home, and it must provide comfort and protection. You should ask an experienced camper to help you choose your tent because it does not follow that the more expensive the tent the better it will be. Make sure it is large enough for the occupants *and* their kit. Although the tent is waterproof it will leak if it is touched when wet or damp so a flysheet is advisable.

Frame tent

A 4-person ridge tent

Lightweight back-pack tent

Groundsheet

Even if your tent is pitched on dry ground, cold and damp rises from the ground at night. A groundsheet is, therefore, essential. The groundsheet must be thoroughly waterproof and should be made from rubber, thick polythene or vinyl plastic (p.v.c.) Many modern tents have sewn-in groundsheets.

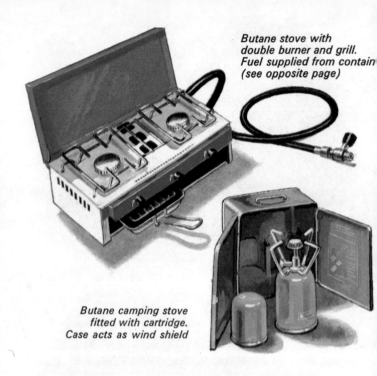

Butane stove with double burner and grill. Fuel supplied from contain (see opposite page)

Butane camping stove fitted with cartridge. Case acts as wind shield

Cooking equipment

There are three principal methods of cooking in camp. What equipment you need will depend on the method you choose.

1 *Over a wood fire* (see pages 24-25 for more details).

2 *With Calor or butane gas stoves:* these are very good for family or motor camping as they are easy and quick to use. They are not however recommended for lightweight or hike camping, since the bottles of fuel are quite heavy.

Unscrew cap of
fuel container

Screw in nozzle
attachment
to stove

**CAMPING
WOODFIRES
ARE _NOT_
PERMITTED**

3 *With pressure stoves:* these should *not* be used by the
novice or young camper as they require care and
experience to use and to maintain. They work on
vaporised paraffin, are light to carry and cheap to
run.

Wherever you choose to camp, first check what types
of fires are permitted, and *always* take great care: fire
is dangerous. Nearly all heath and woodland fires are
caused by carelessly-lit wood fires.

Group equipment

When camping you will need to take all your gear with you—enough to help you to enjoy yourself in comfort. Lightweight campers will take much less, and campers with transport will be able to take more. The following list is suggested as group equipment for four campers. (Your personal equipment check list is at the beginning of the book.)

Kitchen equipment — dixie and nest of three billy cans (large and small camping saucepans); frying pan; kitchen cutlery; buckets and/or polythene water carriers; tin opener; food containers; muslin; washing-up gear (bowl, dishcloth and teatowels, cleansing powder and liquid, scouring pads, etc.); teapot.

Toilets — if there are no toilets at the site(s): a toilet screen complete with pegs, guys, and a small spade or entrenching tool *or* a toilet tent with an Elsan (plus chemical fluid); toilet paper in waterproof container.

General — spare pegs and/or skewers; ball of sisal string; candles; hand axe; bush saw; aluminium foil; assorted ropes; first aid kit (make sure at least one person in your group knows some first aid); matches; maps; mallet; towels.

Optional additional items — collapsable table and chairs; baking tins; compass; small tent for stores.

All gear should be packed neatly and compactly. Hikers should distribute gear among the group according to each person's physical strength, and all campers should know where each item is.

Further information about tents, axes and saws is given later. Particular attention should be given to the method of carrying axes and saws in order to avoid possible accidents.

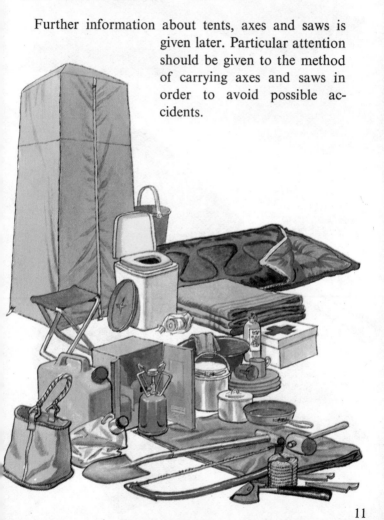

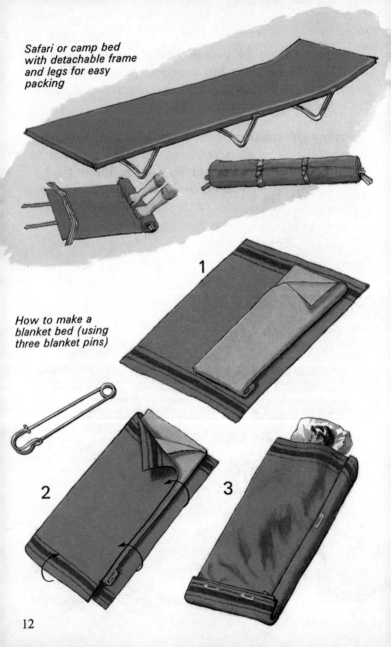

Safari or camp bed with detachable frame and legs for easy packing

How to make a blanket bed (using three blanket pins)

1

2

3

12

Sleeping bag

Bedding

You are much more likely to enjoy yourself if you can keep dry and warm in camp. It is well worth having a camp bed of the safari type which is light and easy to carry. Whether or not you use a bed, always have at least as much bedding—if not more—underneath your body as on top.

The diagrams opposite show you how to make a bed from blankets. For the regular camper a sleeping bag is better than blankets because it is lighter in weight and less bulky. Washable sleeping bags are preferable to those which need to be dry cleaned. *Safety Note:* After a sleeping bag has been dry cleaned it must be well aired, since dry cleaning fumes can be both poisonous and inflammable.

Always have a cotton or nylon inner lining so that you do not have to wash or dry clean your sleeping bag after each camp.

Choosing a camp site

A number of organisations have their own camp sites or approved camp sites, many with toilet and washing facilities. There are also an increasing number of public camp sites. If you do not use one of these you will need to find a camp site of your own. You must always obtain permission to camp on private land. If you wish to camp on common land and other open spaces, make sure that camping is allowed.

Even if you are going to stay for only one night, it is a good idea to take into account the following points before pitching your tent, otherwise you may have an uncomfortable or unpleasant night.

1 Always find a site at least an hour before sunset so that you have time to settle in before dark.

2 The ground should be as level as possible and the soil well drained. Avoid clay and peat. Avoid a site adjacent to the sea, a river or other stretch of water because the air (and possibly the ground) will be damp, and cold.

3 The site should offer some protection from the elements. Choose the leeward* side of a hill, a wood, a hedge, a wall, etc. Never camp in an exposed place.

4 A drinkable water supply should be reasonably close.

5 Beware of natural hazards like dried-up river beds, crumbling rock or earth faces, wild animals (and domestic ones too—cows are inquisitive!), and trees (particularly in thundery weather).

*leeward – the opposite side from which the wind is blowing

Beware of natural hazards . . .

Ideally the site should make you feel at home. Much depends on what *you* like, whether you prefer the company of a lot of other people or whether 'getting away from it all' with family or friends has more appeal.

Geeco water carrier

Jerrycan

Canvas bucket

Collapsable polythene water bottle

Water bottle with webbing harness

Water

Water is essential to life. Without a regular intake of liquid in some form, you would lose weight and eventually die from dehydration and exhaustion. This is most unlikely to happen when camping in the countryside but it is an important point to remember, particularly if you plan to camp in rough or remote terrain and the weather is hot. All water you drink must be pure, however, otherwise you run the risk of becoming ill. If the water is from a mains tap it is probably drinkable, but there are places where water from a tap is not drinkable. If in doubt, check with someone locally.

Water from other sources (such as streams, rivers and wells) should _always_ be treated with caution. Crystal-clear water is not necessarily pure water and cloudy water is not necessarily polluted.

To purify water, you can boil it vigorously for at least five minutes, or you can add one of the special purifying agents which are obtainable from chemists or camping stores. As you become a more experienced camper, you will learn of other methods of water purification which may be used.

Always carry a water bottle with you when on the move, and fill it up whenever you can. In camp, drinking water should always be as fresh as possible, stored in sealed water containers or buckets covered with muslin, and kept in the shade. Never use these containers for anything else.

Water purifying tablets

Boil for five minutes

Store water in shade

Setting up camp

There are usually three main areas in a camp—sleeping tents, kitchen and toilets. Before you start work decide who is going to do what, and what is going to go where.

1 Pitch the sleeping tents with the openings to leeward of the wind direction. Allow enough room between the tents for people to walk without tripping over the guy lines. The tents can be pitched either in a line or, if it is cold, in a semi-circle so that a reflector fire can be made to keep you warm at night. Place a piece of aluminium foil or an upturned tin on the pegs of the four corner guys—these will reflect the beam of a torch at night.

2 The kitchen should be away from the sleeping tents and, if wood fires are used, on the leeward side so that smoke blows away from the sleeping tents. Plan the layout of your kitchen so that everything has its proper place and is easy to use.

3 Toilets: if there are no toilets at the site you will need either a portable toilet which is charged with a sanitary fluid, or you can dig your own. Ask the site owner whether you may dig your own, but never place it close to streams, wells, or trees. Turf the grass carefully (see pages 22-23). The hole should be at least 3 feet deep, 2 feet wide and 1 foot across (1 metre × 60 cms × 30 cms). Place the earth on a sheet of polythene or old canvas beside the trench and provide a trowel. Paper should be kept in a waterproof container. Always wash your hands afterwards. The toilet should be enclosed by a toilet tent or other screening.

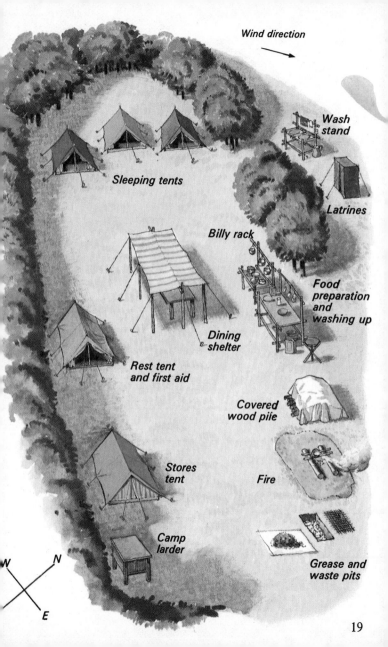

Wind direction

Wash stand

Sleeping tents

Latrines

Billy rack

Food preparation and washing up

Dining shelter

Rest tent and first aid

Covered wood pile

Stores tent

Fire

Camp larder

Grease and waste pits

W N E

19

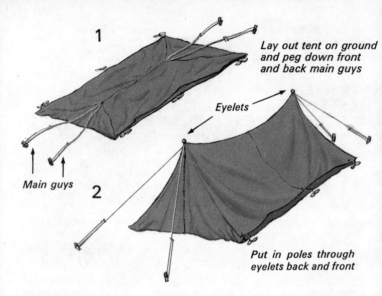

1 Lay out tent on ground and peg down front and back main guys

Eyelets

Main guys

2 Put in poles through eyelets back and front

Pitching a tent

If you have not camped before you will save a lot of time and energy if you practise various camping skills in your back garden or in an open space near your home before you go. Even the smallest tent is easier to pitch if two or more people are doing it. Practise not only on a sunny day but also in wind and rain.

Pitching the tent is very important because unless this is done properly you may either have an uncomfortable night or damage the tent. There is no standard procedure and the one you choose will depend upon the type and shape of the tent you have and the way you find easiest. You will find the following points helpful.

1 The tent doors or flaps should be laced or zipped up. Put the poles together and place the spikes through the eyelets of the tent (and the flysheet) very carefully.

3 *Tighten front and back main guys to keep poles upright to straighten ridge*

4 *Fix side guys and adjust all round until canvas is stretched and ridged*

2 Put in the main guy lines making sure that the pegs or skewers are driven in at an angle of 45°, and the runners come about half way up the line.

3 Fix the side guys in position. The row of pegs should be parallel with the ridge and each guy should always follow the line of the seam to which it is attached. The base of the wall should just touch the ground. Where a flysheet is used place another row of pegs outside the first row so that the flysheet does not touch the tent.

4 Put in the brailing pegs at the foot of the walls.

A well-pitched tent should look neat and tidy with poles straight and secure, and no creases in the fabric.

Turfing

When making a pit in a field for a trench fire, wet and dry pits, toilets, etc., you will first need to cut out a square or rectangle of grass. This is called turfing. Great care needs to be taken so that the turf is removed in neat pieces.

1 Scratch the square or rectangle on the grass for the size of pit or trench you wish to make. Make a cut 2-3 inches (5-7½ cms) deep along the sides with a spade, entrenching tool or knife.

2 Carefully but firmly ease the cutting tool under the grass at one side or end and fold back the turf as you cut.

3 When a whole turf has been cut, take it to a cool, shady place (*e.g.* in a ditch or under a hedge) and sprinkle it with water. The turfs should be watered every day to keep the grass fresh and moist.

4 The trench or pit can now be as deep as necessary. Place all excavated earth on an old sheet of canvas, polythene, or sacking so that it can all be put back in the hole at the end of camp.

Wood fires

Never make a fire near hay or straw stacks, or in or close to dry brush, bracken or undergrowth. Always clear an area at least 10 feet (3 metres) round the fireplace of all leaves, twigs, dry grass, etc. Remember, too, that even a light wind can carry a spark a considerable distance, and never leave embers at night, or when you leave a camp site. Check that wood fires are permitted at each site you use.

Making a wood fire

The illustrations show you how to light a fire. Here are some points to remember when collecting wood for your fire.

1 *Get the right type:* Some wood burns well and some (like elder, willow and chestnut) does not. Never cut or saw live branches off trees or bushes. Collect only dead wood. This will be found under trees and in hedgerows. A *dead* branch can be pulled down from a tree with a rope. Different woods will be needed for starting, developing and maintaining the fire.

To start your fire, always use small pieces—all conifers, hawthorn, and birch. Pine cones come in handy, too. Keep a stock dry in a biscuit tin with a few firelighters and candles so that a fire can be lit in any weather.

To develop it, use birch, holly, and bark from many other trees.

To keep it going, ash, beech, oak, elm, cherry and apple are all useful.

2 *Get the right sizes:* You will need all sizes, but you will need most of a reasonable size to keep the fire going. Learn to use a bush saw and an axe (see pages 26-27).

3 *Get the right quantity:* Always try to have a day's supply of wood so that you do not run out. Avoid collecting so much that you have a lot left over at the end of the camp. Grade the wood into sizes and place it on a sheet of thick polythene or old canvas. Cover the wood pile at night.

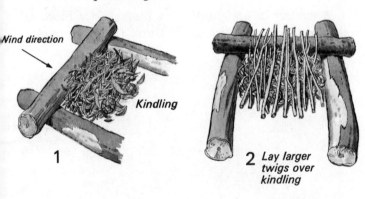

Wind direction

Kindling

1

2 Lay larger twigs over kindling

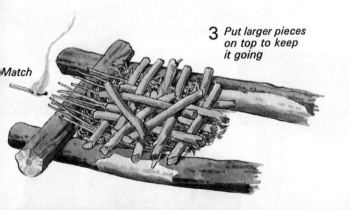

3 Put larger pieces on top to keep it going

Match

The hand axe

Check frequently that the head is secure. Wear strong shoes or boots and remove anything that will get in the way, *e.g.* tie, loose shirt, pendant, etc. Place the wood to be cut on a steady wooden block such as the stump of a tree or a larger log. Get yourself into a comfortable, well-balanced position. Keep other people well away. Hold the grip with one hand and, by bending your arm at the elbow, let the weight of the axe's head do the work.

When not in use either mask the axe in a block as shown, or put it in its sheath. Carry the axe carefully.

The bush saw

Place the wood to be cut on a block or a sawing horse. Grip the saw firmly. Ensure that you are well-balanced to one side of the 'cut' so that you can power the saw from your shoulder. Commence sawing by drawing the blade towards yourself so that a groove is made.

The cutting strokes (whether you are sawing alone or with someone else) are made by the 'pull' and not the 'push' otherwise the blade may snap. Keep the cut as open as possible to prevent jamming. A drop of oil or grease will ease the blade through hard or wet wood.

After use, grease the blade, and mask it with sacking or rubber tube. Keep the saw dry and never leave it lying on the ground.

27

Cooking

Eating in camp does not mean using only tinned and packed foods. Cooking out-of-doors can be just as varied and ambitious as anything prepared in a kitchen at home, but it does need more planning, skill and care. With a gas or pressure stove you will not have as many rings and there may not be an oven. Choose dishes such as stews, hotpots, mixed grills, etc. in which all the ingredients are cooked in the same container. It may be better to have one hot course and one cold one.

Although cooking on a wood fire is not as easy as on a

stove, it does have many advantages. For instance, the fire can be made small for one cooking pot or larger to take several pots; many types of cooking can be done (boiling, steaming, roasting, frying, etc.); and a simple oven can be made. In addition, you can have a supply of constant hot water for washing up and personal washing, and the fire will keep you warm on chilly evenings.

It is very important to light a cooking fire in good time. The best cooking will be done over the steady heat of a bed of hot embers, rather than a fire with a lot of flame and smoke.

Looking after yourself

Personal hygiene is even more important in camping than at home, for out in the open you are more likely to get dirty and to sweat. Your clothes and other gear will need to be looked after properly too.

1 In the mornings when there is dew on the ground or when it is wet, it is advisable to wear plimsolls or sandals without socks, or gum boots and shorts. Wet feet will not harm you but damp socks (or other damp clothes) might.

2 If you do get wet, change into dry clothing as soon as you can.

3 Keep your gear neat and tidy. Store your spare clothes in a rucksack, kitbag or case, and protect the container from rising damp by placing it off the ground, preferably on a rack.

4 Do not pack wet clothes unless you have no alternative and hang out such things as damp towels and face cloths to dry.

5 Have a good wash morning and evening. Scrub your fingernails and ensure that your feet are not only clean but dry as well. Always wash your hands before touching food, before you have a meal, and after you have used the toilet.

6 Have any minor injuries (cuts, scratches, bites, etc.) attended to immediately.

7 Coldness is a camper's worst enemy. Do not wait until you feel cold (particularly in the evening) before putting on an extra sweater. If the weather is good increase your exposure to the sun gradually, so that you do not get sunburn or sunstroke.

Hygiene in the kitchen

Never forget to wash your hands with soap and water before touching food, otherwise the germs on your hands may be transferred to the food you are going to eat. Food should be kept well away from sleeping gear.

Stores Tent It is wise to keep all food separately, preferably in a tent by itself. No food at all should ever be left on the ground. You can make a simple rack a little above ground level on which unopened tins and sacks or bags of vegetables can be stacked. Sugar, biscuits, bread, rice, etc. should be kept in sealed air-tight containers to keep out insects. Keep the stores tent well aired (a length of muslin over the entrance will help to prevent flies, wasps, etc., from getting in) and keep it very clean and tidy.

Camp Larder Fats, milk, meat, fish and other perishable items need to be kept cool, airy and insect proof. It is

possible to buy purpose-made larders and food safes, or you can make your own.

Refuse All rubbish and refuse should be burnt or properly disposed of (*e.g.* in a site dustbin) as soon as possible, since it attracts flies and wasps. If you are using a grease pit, the grass or fern must be burnt at least twice a day, and *always* after the evening meal so a dirty filter is not left overnight. Burn tins and flatten them before putting them in a dustbin or burying them deep in the dry pit.

Left-overs

Wherever possible, do not have any. If you think that some of your food whether cooked or not is going bad, do NOT risk eating it. Any scraps or left-overs should be burnt on a fire, buried and completely covered with earth, or wrapped in newspaper and put in a dustbin.

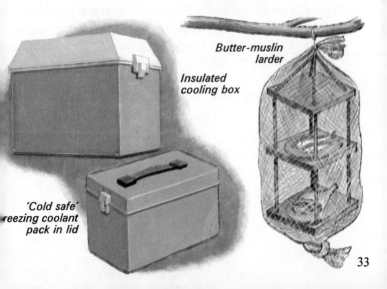

Butter-muslin larder

Insulated cooling box

'Cold safe' freezing coolant pack in lid

Washing up

Few people like washing up, but it is a chore which has to be done and in camp, the sooner it is done the better. Not only will it be easier but also insects are less likely to be attracted. When cooking over a wood fire, pans will become blackened on the outside with smoke. Cleaning will be easier if the outside of the billy or dixie is coated with a paste made from detergent powder and water *or* smeared with washing-up liquid before it goes on the fire.

Wash up everything else with hot water and washing-up liquid, rinse in hot water, and (except for personal utensils) leave to drip dry, covering with muslin, net or cloths to keep out dust and dirt. Containers should be stored upside down. Between meals personal utensils are best kept in a cotton or other bag to keep them clean.

The best way to get rid of dirty washing-up water (also fatty liquids from stews, mince and so on) is to pour it into a *grease pit*. Turf and dig a pit as described on pages 22-3; and cover it completely with twigs and ferns to form a grease trap (which should be burned frequently as mentioned on pages 32-3).

Wash tea towels and dishcloths as often as possible. A dirty tea towel smells sour and is full of germs.

Instructions for diagonal lashing on page 39

Some useful knots

A reef knot is used to join two pieces of string, cord or rope of the same thickness. To tie it, remember "right over left and left over right".

A fisherman's knot is the best way of joining two ropes of equal thickness, particularly if there is a half hitch on either side. It is, however, more difficult to undo than a reef knot.

The sheet bend will be needed to join two lengths of ropes of different thicknesses.

A slip reef is a most useful knot because it is easy to undo. It is ideal for tying up tent brailing, doors, etc.

A *clove hitch* is used to begin and end a square lashing (see pages 38-39), and to fix to a post or pole where the strain is the same on each side.

A *round turn and two half hitches* will secure one end of a rope to a tree, post or pole (that is, where the strain is on one side of the rope).

The bowline is *the* knot for making a loop in the end of a rope because it will not slip. It is widely used in rescues.

A *sheep shank* provides a very useful way of shortening a rope. For a camper this could be used where a guy line, a washing line, etc., is too long. String or rope is always useful and it is better to keep it in lengths which are as long as possible. Two pieces joined together are not as strong as one longer length.

Lashings

A lashing is used to join two poles together with rope. There are many types of lashing, but here are three which a camper will find particularly helpful.

Square lashing

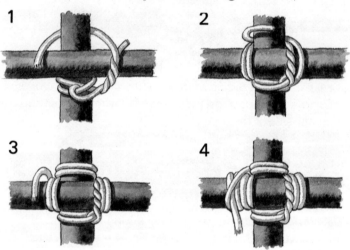

A square lashing is used to secure two poles where they lie at right angles to each other.

1 Tie a clove hitch (see pages 36-37) around the pole which will take the greatest strain and twist the loose end round the rope.

2 Take the working end of the rope *over* the cross pole, behind the upright pole, over the cross pole, etc. Repeat about three times making sure that the rope is pulled tight at each turn.

3 Make the lashing really firm by taking the rope round

the lashing *between* the poles. These are called *frapping* turns. Again, pull the rope tight at each turn.

4 Complete by tying a clove hitch on the second pole.

Diagonal lashing

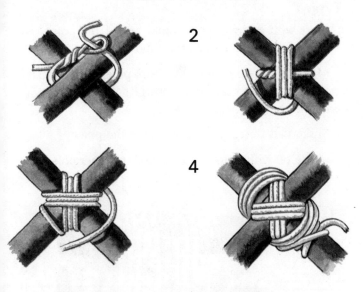

A diagonal lashing is used to secure two poles which are likely to be pulled, or to spring, apart.

1 Commence with a timber hitch.

2 Make three turns following the direction of the timber hitch.

3 Now make three turns round the other fork.

4 Tighten the lashing with two or three frapping turns, and complete with a clove hitch on any of the poles.

Sheer lashing

A sheer lashing is used *either* to form 'legs' from two poles (Type 1) *or* to join two poles together to make a longer pole (Type 2).

Type 1

1 Start with a clove hitch round *one* of the poles (*not* both) and twist the free end round the rope.

2 Make about ten turns round *both* poles; do not make these too tight otherwise you will have difficulty with the frapping turns.

3 Make two frapping turns between the poles.

4 Finish off with a clove hitch round the other pole.

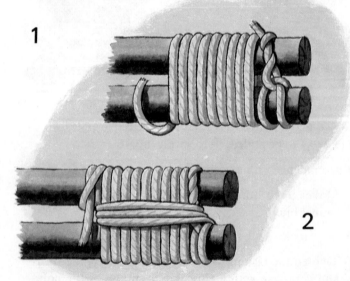

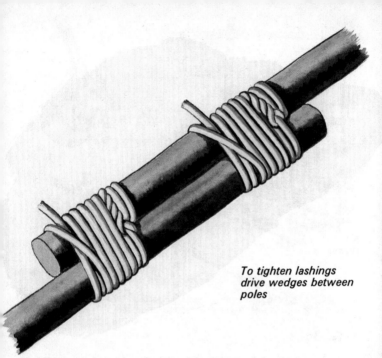

To tighten lashings drive wedges between poles

Type 2

1 Place the two poles to be lashed together side by side. They should overlap by at least a quarter of their lengths, otherwise the extended length will not be firm.

2 Two lashings will be needed, both of which are made in the same way. Start with a timber hitch round *both* poles.

3 Make about ten turns round both poles and finish off with a clove hitch round one or both poles. Do not make any frapping turns.

4 Make a similar lashing at the other end of the overlap.

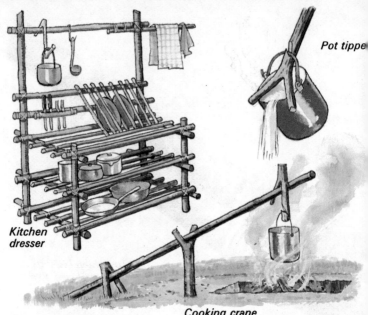

Pot tipper

Kitchen dresser

Cooking crane

Gadgets

A gadget is a device for making life easier, tidier or more comfortable in camp. Although you can buy many gadgets or accessories ready-made, it can become quite expensive, and when you can tie a few knots and lashings you will be able to make most of the camp gadgets you will want from odds and ends, wood, and sisal string.

Wood for gadgets will often be found in hedgerows, copses and woods. Wood which is rotten or which is so dry that it will snap easily is not suitable, but you should not cut living wood from trees, bushes or hedges without the permission of the landowner.

Gadgets can also be made from all sizes and shapes of tin. Great care should be taken when cutting them and

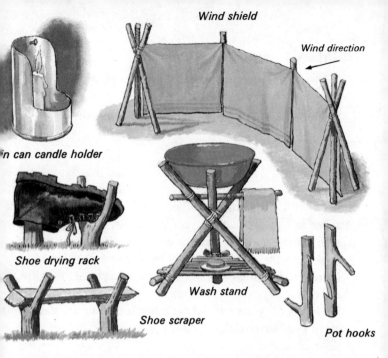

Wind shield

Wind direction

'n can candle holder

Shoe drying rack

Wash stand

Shoe scraper

Pot hooks

jagged edges should never be left but should always be folded over for safety. By cutting sections of rubber bicycle or car inner tubes you will have thick rubber bands which have a wide variety of uses.

Bricks, stones, and wire and all kinds of other junk can also be used to build gadgets.

While the main purpose of a gadget is to help the camper, you will probably get lots of fun from designing and building your own. Hiking or cycling campers who go to remote or rough terrain cannot carry much equipment with them and often rely on the materials they find at their sites. These pictures will give you some ideas to start with.

Safety in camp

You have now read about a number of ways in which you should take care in camp. There are three dangers which need special mention—fire, rain and wind.

Fire

Prevent fires in tents by making sure that lamps are firmly secured away from the tent fabric. Never go to sleep with the lamp on. If possible, don't cook over a stove in the tent where you sleep, but if you have no alternative, make a clear area round the stove, avoid cooking with fats and shield the stove from draughts. Never store inflammable materials such as paraffin, methylated spirit or fuel canisters either inside, or under the eaves of, your tent. Have a bucket of water, sand or earth (or better still, a small fire extinguisher) near the door of each tent.

If a fire *does* start, get everyone out as quickly as you can, pulling people out in their sleeping bags if they cannot easily escape. If the fire is not large either put it out with the fire extinguisher, smother it with a blanket, or cover it with earth or sand. Water must never be used on oil or fat fires. If a fire gets out of hand, wait until everyone is out, then let down the tent by pulling up the guys or kicking out the poles at the bottom. Take down tents on the leeward side to prevent the fire spreading.

When frying with fat, protect your hands by wearing gloves. If a frying pan catches fire, remove it from the fire, cover with a damp (*not* wet) tea towel, and smother with earth or sand.

HUNTERS' FIRE

Wind direction

Always have a clear area of earth round any fire, and never leave embers at night or on leaving the camp site

Using a damp (not wet) tea towel to smother a frying pan which has caught fire

45

Rain

If you have chosen your camp site carefully there should be little chance of your being severely flooded except in extreme conditions. Showers should not cause any real problem as long as you make sure that all your gear is under cover, you have slackened the tent guylines, and you keep yourself dry. If the rain is torrential or continues for some time, it is wise to protect a wood fire with a covering as it will be difficult to restart. To prevent water getting into the tents, dig a trench about six inches deep and six inches wide (15 cm × 15 cm) round the

sides of the tent. The trench should be positioned like the gutter on a house so that water from the tent's eaves or flysheet runs into it. Dig an open channel from the lowest point so that the water can drain away.

If you do get wet, change into dry clothes as soon as possible and dry out your wet clothes at the first opportunity.

Wind

Strong winds can do great damage to your tent. Check and recheck that the guylines are secure and keeping the tent's fabric taut. If the guys work loose the tent will start to flap, loosening the guys even more and the pegs may be ripped out. Close the tent doors to prevent the wind gusting in. In severe gales weigh down the tent walls with stones wrapped in sacking or canvas, and build a windbreak to deflect the airstream over or round the tent.

When you leave a camp site

Whenever you strike camp and leave a site, your two main objectives should be—to clean as much of your equipment as possible so that you do not carry dirty gear; and to leave the site looking so clean and tidy that no one will be able to see that you have been there.

These are the tasks which will need to be done:

1 All remaining refuse, food scraps, litter and other rubbish must be collected and either burned and buried or placed in a dustbin. Tins should be either burned, flattened and buried deep (with the landowner's permission), or put in a dustbin. Bottles and other glass should always be put in a dustbin or taken home.

2 All cooking gear and eating utensils must be thoroughly cleaned (inside and out) in hot water and washing-up liquid, rinsed in hot water and dried well. A thin smear of grease (such as cooking fat) in the seams of cooking pots will be added protection against rust.

3 Dismantle gadgets, etc. Small lengths of string and sticks should be burned if possible. Wood should either be returned to a wood pile or stacked neatly in a convenient place. It is very wasteful to burn wood just because you have collected it. Stone, bricks and other materials should be put in a safe place.

4 When all the washing up has been finished, put out the fire by raking over the ashes and sprinkling on plenty of water. Continue raking and watering until you are certain that the fire is completely out. Move the ashes to the dry pit or to a dustbin. Do not leave them in the fire trench.

5 Fill in all pits and trenches. Tread down the earth *layer by layer*. Replace the turf carefully and water thoroughly.

6 Pack all personal gear not required on the journey. Pack all other equipment, taking particular care that axes, saws, etc. are properly masked and all valves on gas cylinders or canisters are properly turned off.

7 Take down the tents. Whenever possible they should be bone dry before being folded and packed. Any loose earth should be scraped off the pegs and/or skewers which should then be wrapped up separately from the tent. Guy lines should be hanked neatly. If you have to strike camp when the tents are wet or damp, hang them up to dry naturally as soon as you get home. Never place them near direct heat.

8 When you are ready to leave, invite the landowner or warden to inspect your site. In this way you will not only ensure that he is satisfied with your efforts, but you will also leave goodwill behind for other campers who may follow you.

9 As soon as you get home, check through all your gear. Store it away carefully so that it is ready for use on your next camp.

THE COUNTRY CODE

Guard against all risk of fire: A spark can start a raging inferno and cause terrible damage to crops, woodlands and heath.

Fasten all gates: Straying animals can cause harm both to crops and themselves.

Keep dogs under proper control: When near animals or walking along the road, keep your dog on the lead if he cannot be kept under close control.

Avoid damaging fences, hedges and walls: If you force your way through a fence or hedge, you will weaken it.

Leave no litter: Take your picnic remains and other litter home with you.

Safeguard water: It is precious in the country. Never wash dishes or bathe in someone's water supply.

Protect wild life, wild plants and trees: Birds and their eggs, animals, plants and trees should be left alone.

Go carefully on country roads: Country roads have special dangers such as slow-moving farm machinery and led or driven animals. Walk on the right, facing oncoming traffic.

Respect the countryside: Repay the pleasure it has given you by being considerate.